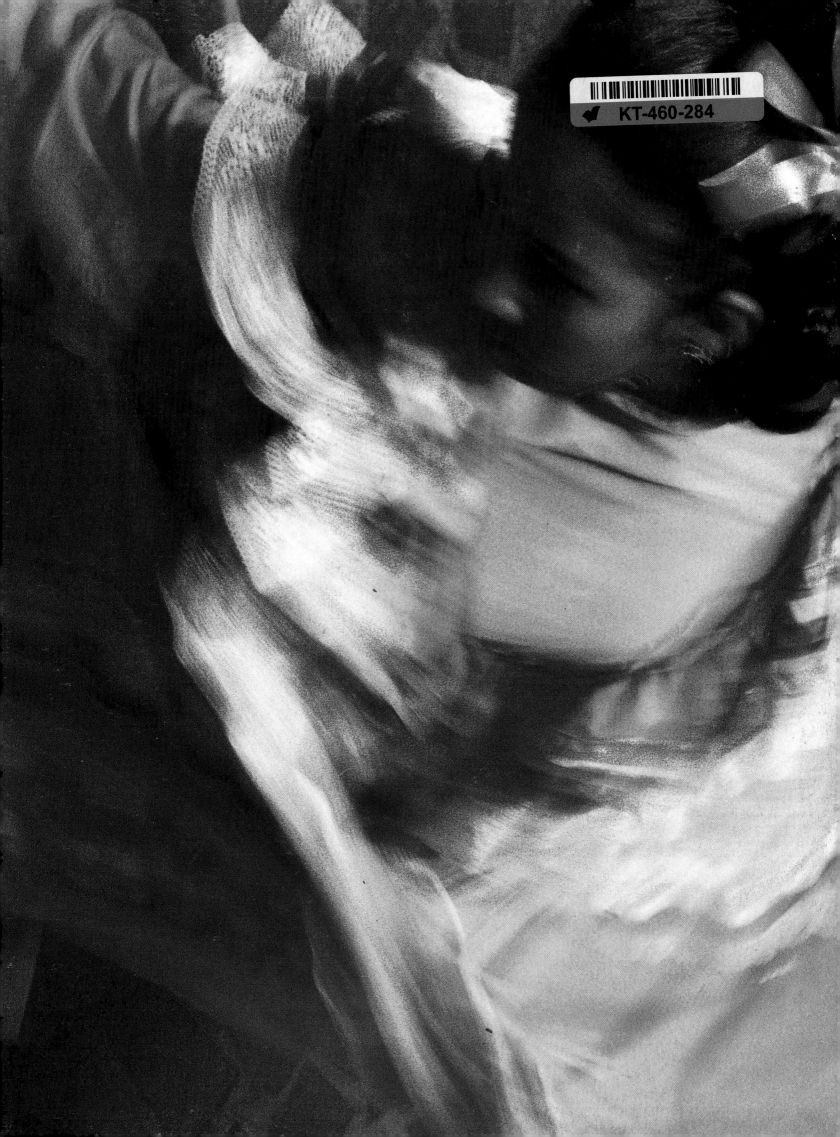

P·I·C·T·U·R·E·P·E·D·I·A

NOTE TO PARENTS

This book is part of PICTUREPEDIA, a completely
new kind of information series for children.
Its unique combination of pictures and words
encourages children to use their eyes to discover and
explore the world, while introducing them to a wealth
of basic knowledge. Clear, straightforward text
explains each picture thoroughly and provides
additional information about the topic.

'Looking it up' becomes an easy task with
PICTUREPEDIA, an ideal first reference for all types of
schoolwork. Because PICTUREPEDIA is also entertaining,
children will enjoy reading its words and looking
at its pictures over and over again. You can encourage
and stimulate further inquiry by helping your child
pose simple questions for the whole family to
'look up' and answer together.

PEOPLE
AND
PLACES

A DORLING KINDERSLEY BOOK
Conceived, edited and designed by DK Direct Limited

Consultant Shane Winser

Project Editor Deborah Chancellor

Art Editor Sonia Whillock
Designer Tuong Nguyen

Series Editor Sarah Phillips
Series Art Editor Ruth Shane

Picture Researcher Lorna Ainger

Production Manager Ian Paton

Editorial Director Jonathan Reed
Design Director Ed Day

First published in Great Britain in 1994
by Dorling Kindersley Limited
9 Henrietta Street
London WC2E 8PS

Reprinted 1997

A CIP catalogue record for this
book is available from the British Library.

ISBN 0-7513-5118-0

Reproduced by Colourscan, Singapore
Printed and bound in Italy by Graphicom

PEOPLE AND PLACES

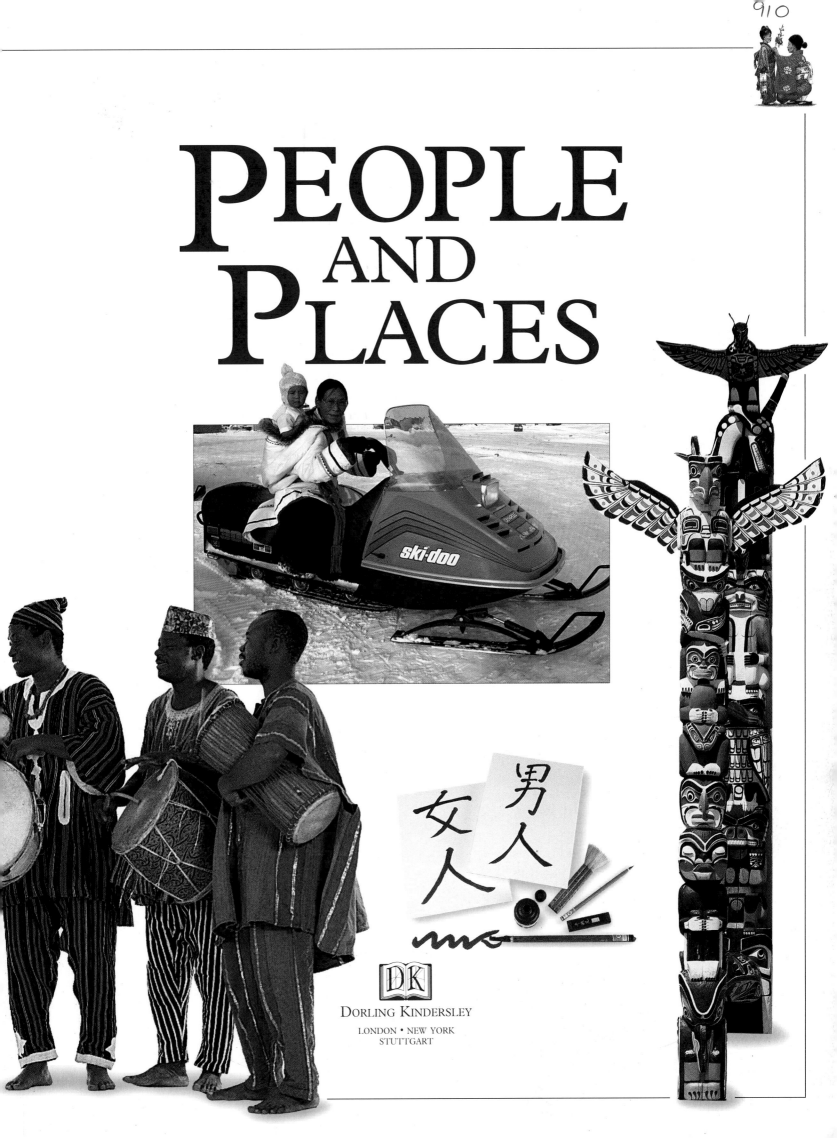

男人
女人

DK

DORLING KINDERSLEY

LONDON • NEW YORK
STUTTGART

CONTENTS

THE ARCTIC & ANTARCTICA

The Inuit people live in the icy lands of the Arctic North. For many generations, they have found practical ways of coping with their cold surroundings. But no one has settled for very long on the southern extremes of the planet. Antarctica is the coldest and windiest place in the world. This huge continent is lashed by freezing blizzards and gales, with temperatures as low as -89°C.

Icy City
Murmansk is a Russian city 200 kilometres north of the Arctic Circle. No other city is farther north than this. The sun does not rise between November and the middle of January.

Homes in the North
In the past, the Inuit were self-sufficient and lived a life on the move, hunting and fishing to survive. They built temporary homes, called igloos, from solid snow. Today, most Inuit live in wooden houses and earn a living by working for other people, often in fish-canning factories or for mining companies.

Long-Lost Relations
For many years, Inuit families on either side of the Bering Strait were not allowed to meet, for political reasons. Nowadays, the North American Inuit and their relations in northern Asia can visit one another once again.

The Arctic

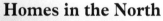

Speedy Ski-Doos
Today, the Inuit people get about on motor sledges, called Ski-doos. This is much faster than using dogs to pull a sledge, which is the traditional method of travel.

Warm clothes are vital in the Arctic.

The Bering Strait is a narrow stretch of sea that separates northern Asia from North America.

Antarctica

Antarctic Science

Scientists from all around the world are the only people who live and work in Antarctica. Some study the effect of the enormous sheet of Antarctic ice on the world's weather patterns. Others observe the behaviour of living things in the freezing conditions.

This scientist is measuring the density of Antarctic snow.

This emperor penguin lives in the Antarctic. No penguins live in the Arctic.

Exploring the Unknown

Antarctica was the last continent to be explored. The first successful expedition in search of the South Pole took place in 1911, led by a Norwegian called Roald Amundsen. The British expedition led by Captain Scott ended in disaster, when the team froze to death on the trek home.

What a Mess

Alaska is an important producer of oil. In 1989, an American oil tanker ran aground just off Alaska, causing one of the world's worst environmental disasters. Over 2,000 kilometres of the Alaskan shoreline were covered with oil.

A windscreen protects the riders from the biting wind.

Runners on the front of the Ski-doo spread the weight of the vehicle evenly, to prevent it sinking into the soft snow.

ski-doo

CANADA

Totem poles often guarded doorways to village homes.

Canada is an enormous country. A journey from the east to the west coast on the world's longest national highway will take you through almost 8,000 kilometres of beautiful landscape. Canada's population of 26 million is small for the country's huge size. Most Canadians live in cities in the warmer southern part of the country, close to the border with the United States.

Some carvings show off the family possessions.

Quebec City

Quebec City is the capital of the province of Quebec. It is Canada's oldest city and the only walled city in North America. Many of its distinctive buildings are in the original French style.

The animals are symbols of the family's ancestors.

Timber!

Half of Canada's four million square kilometres of forest are used for timber. Logging is a very important Canadian industry. On the west coast, large areas of forest are disappearing. Logging companies are being asked to slow down the destruction and to replant more trees.

Modern machinery fells giant conifer trees.

Totem Pole

The Native Americans of British Columbia, on the west coast of Canada, carved giant totem poles out of trees. Some totem poles celebrated special events or the lives of leaders.

Inuit Victory

The Inuit people have lived in the Arctic north of Canada for thousands of years. They have persuaded the Canadian government to give them back control of a large area of their native land. The new territory is called Nunavut and is home to about 17,500 Inuit people.

Is There Anybody Out There?

The first long-distance phone call was made in Canada in 1876. A century later, Canada was the first country to set up a satellite network. Satellites provide a vital link to many remote communities.

Two Languages

Canada has two official languages, English and French. The first Europeans to settle in Canada were the French, followed by the British. Today, the majority of Canadians speak English, but French is the official language in Quebec, Canada's largest province.

Winter Sports

Winters are very harsh all over Canada. Ice hockey and skating are national sports – some families flood their back gardens in winter, so that the water freezes to make a temporary ice rink.

A tug pulls the timber down the river. Water transport is used when there are no major roads through the forest.

The timber is taken to a riverside sawmill, where it is cut into planks or pulped for papermaking.

THE UNITED STATES

The United States is an exciting mixture of different cultures and traditions. Over the last 500 years, about 60 million people from all over the world have made America their home, many entering the country through New York City. The families of the new arrivals now help to make up the American population of about 250 million. The United States is a superpower, and is probably the richest and most powerful nation in the world.

Leading Light

The Statue of Liberty has been a welcoming sight to many immigrants arriving in the United States over the last hundred years. The statue is a symbol of freedom, and was built to celebrate the 100th anniversary of American independence. It was given to the Americans by the French in 1884.

Lots of Languages

Most Americans can trace their family trees back to other parts of the world. Four out of five Americans speak English, but other European and Asian languages are also widely spoken.

Three-quarters of the American population live in cities. This is San Francisco, in the West Coast state of California.

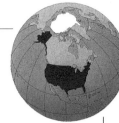

Jean Genie

Jeans are made of tough material called denim.

Jeans are an American invention. The first pair was made in 1874 by Levi Strauss. Levi jeans are still sold all around the world. Today, the jeans industry makes millions of dollars for the American economy.

Drive Time

America is a huge country, and many Americans are used to driving long distances to visit friends or family. Driving is a popular American pastime. Large cars are not as fashionable as they used to be. This is because smaller cars use up less petrol and are better for the environment.

Many American children grow up in suburbs. It is easy to drive from the suburb to the nearest shopping mall or city.

More corn is grown in America than in any other country. Much farming is done by machines, so only three per cent of the labour force work on farms today.

Modern Motorbikes

Today, many Native Americans try to keep up traditional ways and beliefs alongside their modern lifestyles. But many young Native Americans ride motorbikes rather than horses these days!

CENTRAL AMERICA & THE CARIBBEAN

Central America is made up of a narrow strip of eight countries that link the continents of North and South America. Just like the long chain of islands that makes up the Caribbean, Central America is surrounded by clear blue oceans. Today, the beautiful Caribbean Sea and the sunny, sandy beaches attract many tourists.

In the past, the sea brought visitors who were less welcome, like the first settlers from Europe five hundred years ago.

Weaving for a Living

Over half the people of Guatemala are Amerindian. Their ancestors go back a thousand years to the days of the ancient Maya. Guatemala now sells Mayan crafts to the rest of the world.

Horizontal weaving loom

The end of the loom is tied to a tree.

Carnival Time

The Caribbean is famous for its carnivals. For two days and nights at the start of the Christian festival of Lent, people dance through the streets wearing fantastic costumes.

It is often possible to tell which village a weaver lives in from the patterns in her cloth.

A strap around the weaver's back holds the loom steady.

Belize

 Costa Rica **Cuba** **Dominica** **Dominican Republic** **El Salvador** **Grenada** **Guatemala**

 Haiti

  Honduras

 Jamaica

 Mexico

 Nicaragua

 Panama

 St Kitts-Nevis

 St Lucia

 St Vincent and the Grenadines

 Trinidad and Tobago

Pollution City

The four million cars in Mexico City cause awful traffic jams. Pollution from traffic and industry can reach dangerous levels, and mountains around the city stop the bad air escaping.

The Day of the Dead

Every year in Mexico, a festival is held to remember people who have died. It is called The Day of the Dead and takes place at the end of October. Families have picnics by the graves of their relatives. When night falls, they keep watch over the graveyard by candlelight.

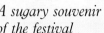
A sugary souvenir of the festival

A Modern Mix

Many Caribbean people are descendants of African slaves, who were forced to work on sugar plantations. Slavery was stopped in the 19th century, and many Asians then came to work in the Caribbean. Their descendants still live there today.

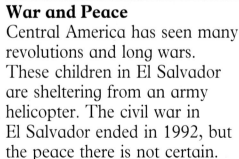

Terrific Temples

Over 1,000 years ago, the ancient Maya peoples built impressive temples, especially in Mexico. Mayan society was very sophisticated long before the Spaniards invaded in the 16th century.

War and Peace

Central America has seen many revolutions and long wars. These children in El Salvador are sheltering from an army helicopter. The civil war in El Salvador ended in 1992, but the peace there is not certain.

Caribbean People

More than fifty different ethnic groups live on the islands of the Caribbean. Here are just a few.

 **Asian**

 Arawak

 **Afro-Caribbean**

 **European**

SOUTH AMERICA

Most South Americans are Roman Catholics. A huge statue of Christ towers over the Brazilian port of Rio de Janeiro. This is a reminder of three centuries of Spanish and Portuguese rule, when the first peoples of South America were almost wiped out. Today, most South Americans still speak Spanish and Portuguese. South America is a growing industrialized area, but many people are still very poor.

Argentina   Bolivia   Brazil   Chile

Galloping Gauchos

Large areas of northern and central Argentina are covered with a grassy plain, called the pampas. Huge herds of cattle are kept on the pampas, and are looked after by cowboys known as gauchos. Most gauchos are descendants of European settlers in South America.

These gauchos from northwest Argentina are wearing traditional Spanish hats and neck kerchiefs.

Stiff, flared leather flaps protect the gaucho's legs from high-growing thistles when he is riding his horse in the pampas.

Heavy leather riding crop

Rich and Poor

São Paulo, in Brazil, is South America's biggest industrial city. The city centre is very modern and wealthy. Many people from the surrounding areas travel to São Paulo in search of work. Their children often end up living in terrible poverty on the streets.

Gauchos are very proud of their horses. They work on ranches called 'estancias'.

A thick poncho is used as a blanket at night. It can also be used as a shield in a fight.

Machu Picchu and La Paz

South Americans have always been clever at building cities high up in the mountains. The ruins of Machu Picchu are hidden 2,280 metres up in the Andes, in Peru. The city was built over 500 years ago, without the help of modern machinery.

La Paz is the capital city of Bolivia. It is the world's highest capital city, 3,636 metres above sea level. The city's steep streets are surrounded by snow-capped mountains. The thin mountain air often makes visitors breathless.

The Yanomami

In 1991, an area of the Brazilian rainforest about the size of Portugal was set aside for the Yanomami tribe. This did not stop miners from invading the land, bringing diseases that have wiped out large numbers of the Yanomami population.

South Americans

South America is a huge continent, with a wide mix of different people.

Highland Amerindian

Lowland Amerindian

South American of African descent

South American of European and Indian descent

NORTHERN AFRICA

The spectacular pyramids and priceless treasures of Ancient Egypt are world famous. Art and culture are still very important to people all over northern Africa. A great range of musical and artistic traditions have been passed down through African families for generations.

The Berber People

Most North Africans are now Muslims. But in Morocco and Algeria, one in five people are still Berbers. Their nomadic way of life has hardly changed for centuries.

The big bass drums are called brekete drums.

Making Music

African rhythms have influenced modern jazz and blues music, and are now an important ingredient of African pop music. These drummers are from Ghana in west Africa.

Famine

Africa has the fastest-growing population in the world. It is hard to grow enough food to feed all these people. Even in a normal year, up to 150 million Africans suffer from a lack of food. When the rains don't come, crops fail and disaster strikes. These children in the Sahel region of northern Africa are in danger of starving.

Egypt
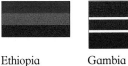 Ethiopia
 Gambia
 Ghana
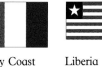 Guinea

Guinea-Bissau
Ivory Coast
Liberia

City Growth

Most Africans live in the countryside, but a steady flow of young men are moving from the villages to look for work in the big cities. Lagos in Nigeria is Africa's fastest-growing modern city.

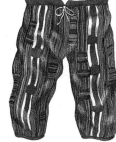

Chocolate Centre

Well over half the world's cocoa is grown in western Africa. More cocoa is grown in the Ivory Coast than anywhere else. About a fifth of Ivory Coast farmland is used to grow cocoa crops.

The drummers' clothes and music come from Dagbon, in northern Ghana.

The smaller drums are called talking drums. The tighter the strings are squeezed, the higher the note.

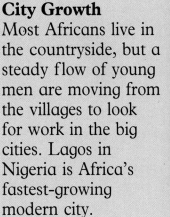

African Crafts

Wood carving, weaving and jewellery making are traditional African crafts.

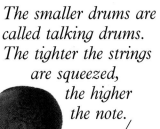

Nigerian wood carving

Narrow-strip woven trousers from Ghana

Bronze bracelet from Mali

Algerian silver jewellery, with enamel decoration

Brass bracelet and earrings from Sudan

 Libya

 Mali

 Mauritania

 Morocco

 Niger

 Nigeria

 Senegal

 Sierra Leone

 Somalia

 Sudan

 Togo

 Tunisia

SOUTHERN AFRICA

Angola

A rich variety of peoples make up the African countries in this region. Huge grassland savannahs support an amazing variety of wildlife. Game parks were first set up in Kenya to protect animals from hunters. Today, these parks are big tourist attractions. Across the whole region, traditional lifestyles, like those of the Kalahari Bushmen, have slowly been replaced with new ways. There have been many personal and political changes for the peoples of southern Africa.

A New Start

The San, or Bushmen, live in the Kalahari desert. For about 20,000 years, they hunted animals and gathered plants to survive. Very few of them still hunt, and most now find work on local farms or in nearby towns.

Today, most Bushmen settle in one place. They have given up a life on the move.

On the Move

Only a few small groups of Bushmen still hunt in the Kalahari desert. Each group has a territory of up to 1,000 square kilometres. The men hunt while the women find tasty fruit, nuts and roots.

Much of the Bushmen's land is now used for farms, cattle ranches and nature reserves.

Botswana

Burundi

Comoros

Congo

Equatorial Guinea

Gabon

Kenya

Lesotho

Madagascar

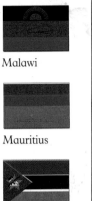

Malawi

Mauritius

Mozambique

Namibia

Rwanda

São Tomé & Príncipe

South Africa

Swaziland

Tanzania

Uganda

Zaire

Zambia

Zimbabwe

Market Day

African women often earn money by selling surplus vegetables from the family farm at the market. Village markets are lively and noisy occasions, where friends meet to exchange the latest news.

Black and White

In 1948, South Africa's white government passed apartheid laws that were unfair to black people. The African National Congress fought the laws, even when Nelson Mandela, their leader, was put in jail. Mandela was let out in 1990. Since then, he has worked hard to end apartheid.

Going to School

Many African children have a long journey to school. A bus takes these Zimbabwean children part of the way, and they have to walk the last few kilometres.

White Tribe

This Afrikaner family lives on a farm in South Africa, near the border with Zimbabwe. They are descendants of the first Dutch South African settlers, who started arriving from Europe in 1652. Like their ancestors, the Afrikaners are still dominant in many aspects of South African life.

Rise of the Zulus

Two hundred years ago, the Zulus were a small clan of a few hundred people, but they fought wars with similar clans to become one big Zulu nation. Today, the Zulus are an important political force in South Africa.

SCANDINAVIA

Scandinavia is the name given to the countries of northern Europe. The far north of this region lies inside the Arctic Circle, so the winters are very harsh. The people of northern Scandinavia enjoy winter sports in the cold climate. Cross-country skiing was invented in Norway, and is still a quick way of getting about during the snowy winter months.

City Slickers
About a quarter of the Danish population live in Copenhagen, the capital of Denmark. Most Scandinavians choose to live in cities in the warmer south of the region.

Sweat It Out
Saunas are wooden rooms, steaming with heat from a stove. Invented in Finland over 1,000 years ago, they are found in many homes in Scandinavia. After a sauna, people often enjoy a cold shower or a roll in the snow.

Escape to the Country
Many Scandinavians enjoy a high standard of living. Some can afford to buy or rent a second home in the mountains, in the forest, or by the sea. They escape to these 'holiday huts' at weekends and during the summer months.

Land of the Midnight Sun
Imagine waking at midnight, to find the sun shining outside! At the height of summer, the tilt of the Earth causes northern countries to get more of the sun's light. In northern Scandinavia, it doesn't get dark at all in the middle of summer.

It is still light at midnight, because the sun hasn't set.

Dark Days
It is the middle of winter, and the people in this northern Scandinavian town are eating midday lunch in the dark! In winter, the tilt of the Earth causes countries in the far north to get less of the sun's light. Days get shorter, until the sun doesn't rise at all.

| Denmark | Finland | Iceland | Norway | Sweden |

Out in the Cold
The Saami, or Lapp people, are traditionally a nomadic group, travelling throughout northern Scandinavia and Russia herding their reindeer. It is getting harder and harder to make a living in this way, so many young Saami are now becoming fishermen and farmers.

Legoland
Denmark is the home of Lego, one of the world's most popular children's building toys. A theme park has been built entirely from Lego bricks near Billund. It is now a big tourist attraction.

Lego giraffe

Earthly Energy
These Icelanders are swimming in waters warmed by energy deep under the Earth. This geothermal energy is also used to generate electricity and heat houses.

At midday, the hot sun is at its highest position in the sky.

At seven o'clock in the morning, the sun is already well up in the sky.

It is six o'clock, and the long, light evening is just beginning.

THE BRITISH ISLES

The Republic of Ireland is an independent country, with its own government and traditions. England, Scotland, Wales and Northern Ireland make up the United Kingdom. Many aspects of British life, such as its historical buildings and customs, have been preserved. But the United Kingdom is also good at adapting to change. A rich variety of ethnic groups now live in the United Kingdom's multicultural society.

Beside the Seaside
Britain is surrounded by the sea. British seaside holidays first became popular in the 19th century. Today, many British people go on holiday abroad, where it is less likely to rain!

The Oldest Democracy
The Houses of Parliament in London have been the home of British democracy since 1512. The political party with the most representatives, called MPs, forms the government. MPs are voted in at national general elections.

The Commons' Chamber is where the 651 MPs debate government decisions.

Howzat!
Sunday afternoons in summer would not be the same in many English villages, without the familiar sight of a cricket match on the village green. Cricket is an English invention, and is usually followed by another well-known English tradition, afternoon tea!

Big Ben is named after the huge bell in the clock tower.

Guy Fawkes Night
A plot to blow up the Houses of Parliament almost succeeded in 1605, but the ringleader, Guy Fawkes, was caught and executed. Guy Fawkes Night is still celebrated all over England on November 5, when home-made straw dummies – called guys – are burnt on big bonfires at firework parties.

Republic of Ireland   United Kingdom

Arty Edinburgh

For three weeks every August, a big arts festival takes place in Edinburgh, the historic capital of Scotland. The festival gives amateur and part-time entertainers the chance to perform, and also attracts some of the world's best musicians, theatre companies and artists.

Foot-Tapping Folk

Traditional folk music is extremely popular in Ireland. The accordion is a typical folk instrument, often played to accompany singers. Irish bands have been very successful on the world pop scene. Many songs were first written in Gaelic, the original language of Ireland.

Possible new laws are debated in the Lords' Chamber.

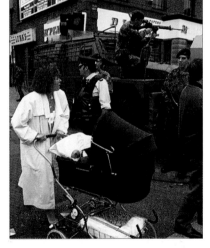

A Divided Community

Northern Ireland is part of the United Kingdom, but is divided along religious lines. The Protestant majority want to stay under British rule, while the Catholic minority want to join the Republic of Ireland. Police and the British Army try to keep the peace in this violent conflict, while ordinary people try to carry on with their lives.

National Pride

The Welsh are proud of their culture, and enjoy celebrating national festivals. St David is the patron saint of Wales, so on St David's Day, children go to school wearing traditional Welsh costume.

The leek is the national emblem of Wales.

23

FRANCE & THE LOW COUNTRIES

The Netherlands, Belgium and Luxembourg are sometimes called the Low Countries, because much of the land is flat and low-lying. France and the Low Countries are powerful farming and trading nations, thanks to their good soil and large natural harbours. The people of the region are fond of good food. French chefs are world famous for their fine cooking skills.

European Dream
The stars on the European Community flag represent its 12 members, which are Belgium, Denmark, France, Germany, Greece, Italy, Luxembourg, the Netherlands, Portugal, the Republic of Ireland, Spain and the United Kingdom.

This stylish outfit is by Christian Lacroix, a top French fashion designer.

Style Capital
Paris, the capital of France, is at the heart of the world fashion industry. Every season, famous designers display new creations at big shows.

Chocolate Secrets
Many Belgian chocolate makers keep their recipes secret, so no one can copy them.

Brandy

Coffee

Mint

Nougat

Mixed nuts

City Canals
Amsterdam is the capital of the Netherlands. It is built around a network of canals that were once used for trade and transport. By tradition, the Dutch find their way about the city on bicycles.

At War with the Sea
Nearly half of the Netherlands was once under sea water. Over the centuries the Dutch have reclaimed this land from the sea, draining it by using a clever system of canals and sea walls, or dykes. Much of the reclaimed land is now used for intensive crop and dairy farming.

Land of Wine

France produces some of the world's best wines. Each region has its own wines, with their own special flavours. In the Rhône valley in southeast France, grapes ripen in the summer sun. They are then harvested and fermented in vats.

Fabulous Food

The French love their food, and take care to buy it as fresh as possible. Most French people are careful shoppers, closely inspecting food and even sampling it before they buy.

Attractive vegetable displays are arranged to catch the shopper's eye.

Many French shops sell only one kind of produce, but offer a wide range of choice.

Small But Rich

Luxembourg is a tiny country that nestles between France, Belgium and Germany. Its small population has a high standard of living, because of the country's success as a financial centre.

Crusty French bread is bought every morning, as it does not keep fresh for long.

SPAIN & PORTUGAL

Both Spain and Portugal have warm, sunny climates and long coastlines. The blue skies and dazzling white beaches of Spain's Mediterranean coast attract millions of tourists every summer. The sea is also an important source of food and employment. Fishing is a major industry in Portugal and on Spain's Atlantic coast.

Young Spaniards can ride scooters from the age of 14.

Easy Riders

Scooter-riding is a craze for young people in many parts of Spain, especially the regions of Valencia and Catalonia. Bikers meet in the evenings, to compare bikes and arrange races.

This scooter can reach a top speed of 95 kilometres an hour.

Fiesta!

Spain has more festivals than any other European country. Some are religious – others are just for fun. One of the messiest festivals takes place in Bunyols, in Valencia. The villagers pelt each other with tomatoes, to celebrate the time when a lorry spilled its load of overripe tomatoes all over the village square.

Tide of Tourists

Mediterranean countries are very popular with tourists. In 1990, 170 million tourists flocked to the coasts of southern Europe. Every year, the Spanish population doubles when tourists arrive to enjoy the hot summer weather and sandy beaches.

Andorra   Portugal   Spain

Take Your Pick

These Portuguese farmers grow oranges, lemons and olives, and are especially proud of this year's crop of oranges. Orchards of sweet, juicy oranges are a common sight in the hot countryside of southwest Portugal.

City of Seven Hills

Lisbon, the capital of Portugal, is the smallest capital in Europe. It is built on seven steep hills. Old electric trams carry the townspeople up and down the sloping streets.

Eating Around Spain

Here are some tasty dishes from different regions of Spain.

Gazpacho – cold tomato soup from Andalusia

Fire Dance

Flamenco dancing was developed many hundreds of years ago by the gypsies of Andalusia. It is still popular all over Spain. Many Spanish children learn the dance from a young age, and enjoy wearing the colourful flamenco costumes.

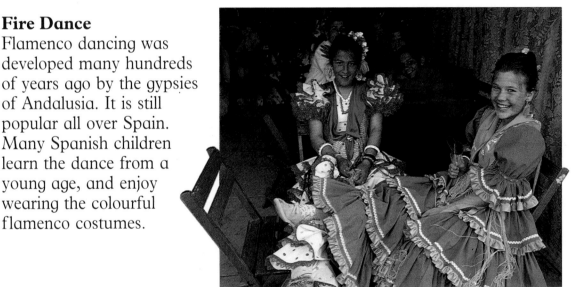

Cocido – meat stew from Castile and Estremadura

Zarzuela de Pescado – seafood stew from Catalonia

Paella – chicken, seafood and rice from Valencia

First Communion

Most Spanish people are Roman Catholics. From the age of seven or eight, children are taught the main beliefs of the Catholic church, ready to take their first communion at the age of ten. The ceremony is a religious and social occasion – an important event for all the family.

Doughnuts – a popular sweet all over Spain

GREECE & ITALY

Greece and Italy lie in southern Europe, where the warm summers and beautiful Mediterranean coastline draw millions of tourists every year. Many magnificent buildings, dating back to the days of the Ancient Greeks and Romans, are also popular attractions. A lot of these sites are in urgent need of repair. Both Greece and Italy are struggling to keep their ancient monuments in good condition.

Priests on Parade
Greek Orthodox priests are allowed to get married, unlike Roman Catholic priests. Priests play an important part in both Greek and Italian society and are given great respect.

Café Talk
In some parts of Greece and Italy, far away from the busy towns and cities, life carries on at a very relaxed pace. Many families rest in the strong heat of the day. In the cooler evenings, men often gather in cafés for a drink and a chat.

Chemicals from car exhausts are eating away at the ancient stone.

Parts of the Parthenon have been so badly damaged, they need to be restored or replaced.

So many tourists visit the Parthenon that its steps are being worn away.

Temple under Threat
The Parthenon in Athens is an ancient Greek temple, built to honour Athene, the goddess of wisdom. It is now under threat from air pollution and the tramping of millions of visitors' feet.

Cyprus	Greece	Italy	Malta	San Marino	Vatican City

The Pope's City

The Pope is head of the Roman Catholic Church. He lives in a tiny country called the Vatican City, which lies within the walls of Rome, the capital of Italy. This state has its own laws, police force and even its own postal service!

Car Italia

The Fiat car works, in Turin northern Italy, is one of the largest car factories in the world. Over 140,000 people work there to make more than one and a half million cars every year.

Pasta Preparations

More types of pasta are made in Italy than anywhere else in the world. Flour, eggs, vegetable oil and salt are mixed to make dough, which is then rolled out and cooked. Pasta is often eaten with a tasty sauce.

Spaghetti Bolognese

Big arches reduce the weight of this typical Venetian building.

Brick foundations are laid on wooden posts, which are driven deep into the mud.

Grand Passions

Opera and soccer are two of Italy's top obsessions. The soccer World Cup took place in Italy in 1990. Luciano Pavarotti, the world-famous Italian opera singer, sang at a gala concert to celebrate this important tournament.

Sinking City

Venice was built over 300 years ago on the mudbanks of a lagoon on Italy's northeast coast. The floating city is slowly sinking. Many of its buildings have been damaged by pollution and constant contact with water, and need to be carefully restored.

GERMANY, AUSTRIA & SWITZERLAND

Germany, Austria and Switzerland lie at the heart of Europe. Central Europeans share a love of traditional food, drink and festivals. They also share a language, as German is the most widely spoken language of the region. Germany is a powerful country. After years of separation for political reasons, East Germany rejoined West Germany in 1990 to become one big country. The wall dividing East from West Berlin was torn down amidst great celebrations.

Fantasy Castle

The castle of Neuschwanstein nestles among the Bavarian Alps in south Germany. It was built about a hundred years ago by a rich Bavarian king with a wild imagination.

Tall turrets give the castle a fairy-tale appearance.

King Ludwig II died in 1886, before this spectacular castle was finished.

Starting School

German children start primary school at the age of six, although most have been to a nursery, or kindergarten, for three years before this. On their first day, children are sent to school with a large cone stuffed with everything they will want, including sweets, pens and books.

The castle attracts tourists from all around the world.

Austria   Germany   Liechtenstein

Switzerland

Coming Down the Mountain

The return of cows from the Alps is celebrated in August. It is called the Einabtrieb. The cows are usually decorated in bright colours. But if somebody has died, the decorations are black or dark blue.

Snowy Holiday

Every year, thousands of skiers visit resorts in Austria and Switzerland. Some people worry that mountain tourism spoils the environment. But it brings lots of money for both countries and is a big employer of local people.

Very Viennese

One in five Austrians lives in Vienna, the capital of Austria. The city was once at the centre of the great Austro-Hungarian empire. It is still an important city, and is the home of many United Nations organizations.

The highest point of the wheel is nearly 65 metres above the ground.

Each carriage takes up to 12 passengers.

The Biggest Wheel

The Riesenrad in Vienna is one of the largest big wheels in the world. The wheel is 61 metres across, and it turns round at the slow speed of 75 centimetres a second.

Three Languages

Switzerland is surrounded by Germany, Austria, Liechtenstein, France and Italy. Three main languages are spoken in Switzerland – French, German and Italian. Most Swiss people speak German, but many speak at least two of these languages.

EASTERN EUROPE

Eastern Europe has been invaded many times, and is now a meeting place for many different cultures and religions. The breakdown of Communism during the 1980s and 1990s has brought new freedom to the region, but has also allowed back old tensions between many of the ethnic groups.

War Torn

A wide mix of people used to live together peacefully in the former Yugoslavia. At the end of the 1980s, war broke out between the different ethnic groups. A once beautiful European country has now been torn apart by the conflict.

Czech Cartoons

Children's films from Slovakia and the Czech Republic are world famous. This Czech film shows a typical mix of live action and puppet animation.

Royal Romanies

The Romany people are also called gypsies. This group is the 'royal family' of the gypsy king of Romania. There may be well over 250,000 gypsies in Romania.

The Romanies are one of the biggest minority groups in Romania. This man is the king of the Romanian gypsies.

Gypsies have always been independent, refusing to live in cities and change their travelling way of life.

Albania

Bosnia and Herzegovina

Bulgaria

Croatia

Czech Republic

Hungary

Macedonia

Poland

Romania

Slovakia

Slovenia

Yugoslavia

Dracula's Castle

A Romanian prince, Vlad Tepes, who lived in this castle over 500 years ago, inspired the story 'Dracula'. This story about a scary, bloodsucking vampire is not true. But the real prince who lived here in the Transylvanian Alps was indeed a cruel man, who killed all his enemies.

Hungarian Farming

Farms like this one in Hungary cover three-quarters of the country's land. Modern farming methods have not yet reached much of eastern Europe. Crops have been harvested in the same way for many generations.

Favourite Foods

Some typical eastern European dishes.

Cherry soup

Sauerkraut

Goulash

Apple strudel

Many gypsies speak Romany, which is similar to some north Indian languages.

City of Learning

Cracow was once the capital of Poland, and its streets are lined with many beautiful buildings. Cracow is Poland's oldest university city, founded over 600 years ago.

Pollution Problem

Many countries in eastern Europe suffer from bad pollution. Not enough money is spent on modernizing old factories. Foreign industries have set up new factories, but some of these have made the pollution problem even worse.

THE MIDDLE EAST

The discovery of oil has made parts of the Middle East very rich and powerful. Huge oil refineries are a common sight in the region. But the oil will not last for ever, and other industries are being developed to keep the money coming in when the oil has run out. The Middle East has always been a very productive area. Its age-old civilizations have exported farming techniques, beautiful crafts and three major religions all around the world.

Desert Survivors
This family lives on the edge of the desert in Oman. They belong to a group of travelling Arabs called the bedouin. For 4,000 years, nomadic bedouin have survived in the hottest parts of the Middle East, leading camels and goats in search of water and pasture.

Bedouin women dress modestly in traditional masks and black overdresses.

Turkish Bazaar
In the Middle East, many people shop in markets and bazaars. This shopkeeper is hoping to sell some of his brassware at the Great Covered Bazaar in Istanbul, Turkey.

Bedouin girls wear colourful clothes and silver and gold jewellery.

It's a Camel's Life
Most bedouin families own a pick-up truck. These do much of the work once done by camels. Camels are prized as symbols of wealth. A camel may be sold to a camel racer for several thousand dollars.

Living on a Kibbutz
In Israel, big farms, called kibbutzim, were set up so many Jewish families could live and work on the same farm and share the produce.

A decorative silver dagger is a sign of power and wealth.

White clothes reflect bright sunlight and help people keep cool.

Bedouin men and boys wear head shawls to protect their heads from the sun. In June, the Omani desert can reach 45°C in the shade.

The Dome of the Rock

City of Faith
Jerusalem is a special city for Jews, Christians and Muslims. Jews come to pray at the Wailing Wall, on the site of the Old Temple. Christians believe Christ came back to life after his death in Jerusalem. The Dome of the Rock marks the spot where Muslims believe Muhammad rose to heaven.

The Wailing Wall, where Jews go to pray.

Trip of a Lifetime
At least once in a lifetime, every Muslim must try to make a special journey, or Hajj, to Mecca in Saudi Arabia. During the Hajj, visitors crowd into the Great Mosque, and walk seven times around the shrine, called the Ka'ba.

Afghanistan

Bahrain

Iran

Iraq

Israel

Jordan

Kuwait

Lebanon

Oman

Qatar

Saudi Arabia

Syria

Yemen

United Arab Emirates

Turkey

NORTHERN EURASIA

Northern Eurasia stretches across a vast area, from Ukraine in the west to the frozen wastes of Siberia. For centuries, northern Eurasia has been controlled by powerful rulers and governments. But in recent years, the communist Soviet Union has split into 15 independent states. Mongolia had close links with the former Soviet Union, but was never part of it.

Daring Dance
This energetic dance celebrates the courage of cossack soldiers from the Ukraine.

Rocking Russia
These rock fans are enjoying a concert in Moscow, the capital of Russia. Big changes happened for the Russians in the late 1980s. Strict communist rules were relaxed and the people began to enjoy new freedoms.

Going to Church
Orthodox Christianity has been the traditional Russian religion for over 1,000 years. The cathedral of St Basil is one of the most spectacular Russian Orthodox churches.

The cathedral lies in Red Square, right in the heart of Moscow.

St Basil's was built for Tsar Ivan the Terrible in the 1550s, to mark his military successes.

Keeping the Faith
The Communist Party disapproved of all religions. The Jews suffered badly – their synagogues and schools were closed down. Jewish traditions survived, but they are now practised mainly by older people.

High Fliers
The circus is a popular form of entertainment all over Russia. One of the most famous circuses in the world is based in Moscow. The New Moscow Circus boasts a high standard of acrobatics. Its grand Big Top was opened in 1971 and seats an audience of up to 3,400 people.

Northern Eurasians
The largest ethnic group of northern Eurasia is made up of Slavs. Next biggest is the Turkic-speaking population. Smaller groups include Mongols and Inuit.

Ukrainian Slav

Eastern Promise
The people of Central Asia look very different from the Russians who live farther north. They speak languages similar to Turkish and many are Muslims, like their neighbours in the Middle East. These women are selling bread at a market stall in Uzbekistan.

Turkic-speaking
Uzbek

Colourful onion-shaped domes top the nine chapels of St Basil's.

Yesterday's Hero
Ancestors of these Mongol horsemen fought in the army of the fierce Mongol emperor, Ghengis Khan, 1,000 years ago. Today, Ghengis Khan is once again a Mongolian national hero.

Mongol

Ripe Old Age
This Azerbaijani couple married 102 years ago, and have 190 descendants! A lifetime of fresh mountain air and a healthy diet of honey, herbs and dairy food has seen them well into old age.

Russian Inuit

CHINA, HONG KONG & TAIWAN

There are more than 200 million bikes in China, so cycling in the rush hour can be very slow! There are more people in China than in any other country – over a billion people live and work in this amazingly varied land. Fifty-seven different ethnic groups make up the population, but by far the largest group is the Han, traditionally a peasant farming people.

Communism in China
The Communist government in China plays an active role in people's everyday lives. This official government poster encourages couples to have only one child.

Food and Farming
Two-thirds of the Chinese people are farmers, growing crops on every spare patch of suitable land. Up to three crops of rice may be grown on the same paddy field each rice-growing season.

Rice is the basic food for China's huge population.

Bringing up Baby
The 'one child per family' rule was introduced in 1979 to try to control the fast population growth. It was needed to keep the Chinese population under 1.2 billion by the year 2,000.

Words and Pictures
The Chinese written language is based on pictures, which describe objects, actions and ideas. There are about 50,000 pictures, or characters. A simplified list of about 2,000 is commonly used today.

男人
Man

女人
Woman

Lettering brush

China   Taiwan

Folk Art in Taiwan

Taiwan has some colourful folk traditions. A sticky mixture of rice and flour is dyed and moulded to make these decorative figures. In the past, the flour and rice recipe was used to make children's snacks. Today, the figures are kept, not eaten.

Hong Kong

Nearly six million people live in the 1,045 square kilometres of Hong Kong, making it the world's most crowded place. Hong Kong is a busy trading centre and the world's biggest exporter of watches, clocks and toys.

Many Chinese people would like to be allowed to have bigger families. It is hard for them not to spoil their 'only' children.

Get Well Soon

This street trader is selling herbal medicines. Ancient, natural ways of treating illnesses are very common in China.

Angelica root

Most Chinese mothers are in full-time work. Their children are looked after in creches at the workplace, until they are old enough to go to to school.

Buddhist Tibet

Most people living in Tibet are Buddhists. They believe their past leaders are alive now in the body of their present leader, the Dalai Lama. In 1959, the Dalai Lama fled his home, the Potala Palace, to escape the invading Chinese army. He now lives in exile in India.

JAPAN & KOREA

Japan is famous for its electronic gadgets and machines. In the last 35 years, Japan has become one of the world's richest countries, and many Japanese people enjoy a high standard of living. Japan's neighbour, Korea, is split into two separate countries. North Korea has cut off its links with the South and is one of the world's most secretive societies. South Korea is a successful industrial country, like Japan, and trades with the rest of the world.

Fish Food
The traditional Japanese diet of fish is very healthy. Many Japanese people live to be very old – in 25 years' time, about a quarter of the population will be elderly.

Children on Parade
The Seven-Five-Three Festival in Japan is named after the ages of the children who take part. Every year on November 15, girls and boys are dressed up in traditional costume and taken to a Shinto shrine. It is a very sociable occasion.

Dinner Time
The evening meal is an important time for busy Japanese families to get together and relax. Parents often get home late from work, and children have lots of homework to do in the evenings.

Rice is cooked until it is sticky, so it is easy to eat with pointed chopsticks.

An electric rice cooker sits close to the table.

Japanese tea is drunk without milk, and is called green tea.

Mind Your Head
These pupils are not hiding from their teacher! They are practising what to do if there is an earthquake. Earthquakes do not happen often in Japan, but they could happen any time. In the past, they have caused terrible damage.

書店

Japan

North Korea

South Korea

Colourful Koreans
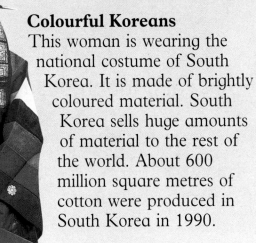
This woman is wearing the national costume of South Korea. It is made of brightly coloured material. South Korea sells huge amounts of material to the rest of the world. About 600 million square metres of cotton were produced in South Korea in 1990.

The food is placed on the table before the family sits down to eat.

The family sits on cushions around a low table to eat their meal.

Selling Ships
Most of the ships in Asia are made at the Hyundai shipyard in South Korea, the biggest shipyard in the world. In 1990, 35 big ships were built at the yard – altogether, they weighed a massive 1.8 million tonnes.

Watch This Space
The big cities of Japan can get extremely crowded. Space is often very hard to come by, but the smallest places are always put to good use. This shopkeeper has hundreds of personal stereos for sale in a tiny kiosk in Tokyo.

Chopstick rest

Presentation is very important with Japanese cookery. Portions are always small and dainty.

Climb Every Mountain
Japanese people work hard, but they also enjoy their hobbies. Japan has some stunning mountain ranges, and many Japanese people keep fit with mountain climbing. These hikers are up Mount Furano-Dake, on the island of Hokkaido in north Japan.

書店

The Indian Subcontinent

The Indian subcontinent includes India, Sri Lanka, Pakistan, Bangladesh, Bhutan and Nepal. Most people in this part of the world follow the Hindu, Muslim or Buddhist religions. In India, eighty per cent of the huge population are Hindus. Every year, millions of Hindus make pilgrimages to the holy city of Varanasi in north India, to wash away their sins in the River Ganges.

Country Life

Eight out of ten Indians live in small country villages. Cows are kept in each one, and the human population is only three times bigger than the cow population! Hindus believe that cows are holy, so they don't eat them. According to Hindu teaching, 330 million Hindu gods and goddesses live in the body of a cow.

The bride is nine years old. After the wedding she will return to her family until she is old enough to live with her new husband.

The beautiful wedding sari is made of expensive silk.

The people in this village make combs for a living.

Hindu Theatre

The Dusserah festival celebrates the end of the rainy monsoon. Groups of actors perform episodes from the story of Ram, a Hindu god in human form. The main parts are played by the top class of Indian society, called the Brahman caste.

Wedding Day

Most Hindu parents choose the person their son or daughter will marry. It is important that the partner they pick belongs to the right class, or caste, of Indian society. Children are often engaged and married when they are quite young. Their weddings are colourful and happy family occasions.

Bangladesh

Bhutan

India

Maldives

Nepal

Pakistan

Sri Lanka

The bride's family gives expensive presents to the groom's family. This is called the dowry.

The groom is eleven years old. He is leading his bride to the marriage ceremony.

Floods in Bangladesh

Bangladesh is a very low, flat country, criss-crossed with rivers. After heavy rain, flooding can cause terrible damage. This farmer is helping to push a tricycle taxi, called a rickshaw, through a flooded village in northeastern Bangladesh.

Climb Every Mountain

The Sherpa people of Nepal live high up in the Himalayas. Many Sherpas earn money by guiding tourists, trekkers and mountaineers up the steep and rocky paths.

Women at the Top

Most people in Pakistan are Muslims. In 1988, Benazir Bhutto was voted the first woman prime minister of a Muslim country. In 1993, she was elected for the second time.

Red-Hot Spice

Curry is a very popular Indian dish, and is enjoyed all around the world. Spices are important ingredients in a curry.

Lentils

Coriander

Ginger

Naan bread

Spicy potatoes

Lamb curry

SOUTHEAST ASIA

It is hard to get away from water in most parts of Southeast Asia! The ten countries that make up the region are linked by waterways and surrounded by oceans. The hot, wet environment is ideal for farming rice, the staple crop of the region. It also supports large areas of tropical rainforests. Sadly, heavy logging has forced many forest people to move away to towns, where the way of life is very different.

People Power

The Penan people live in the rainforests of Sarawak. They have tried to stop the destruction of their forest home by blocking roads into the rainforest. Sarawak has the world's highest rate of logging.

The Secret of Success

The small island state of Singapore is a powerful trading nation. Singapore became successful because of its position. It was built up as a key trading post between the Far East and the West, and is now one of Asia's richest countries.

Living with Water

Many houses in Malaysia and Indonesia are built on stilts. This helps protect them from floods during torrential rainstorms.

The houses are called 'long' houses. Behind each door is a large room, or 'bilik', where the family lives.

The houses are made both from natural and modern materials. Some roofs are made from palms, others from corrugated iron.

Cambodia

Indonesia

Laos

Malaysia

Philippines

Singapore

Thailand

Vietnam

Bali Dancers

The Indonesian island of Bali is famous for its exciting dances. Historical tales of local princes and heroes are acted out in a masked dance called the Wayang Topeng. The dance is very entertaining, with lots of clowning about as well as serious storytelling.

Floating Market

Much of Bangkok in Thailand is below sea level, and the city has a busy network of canals. Floating markets are colourful occasions – local traders bring their goods to market by boat, and shoppers paddle up to take a look at what is on offer.

A Topeng dancer acts out the character of the mask.

Every movement is carefully controlled.

Doing Time

The vast majority of Thais are Buddhists. Every male Buddhist is expected to become a monk for a while, to study religious teachings and prepare for adult life.

Pirates on the South Seas

Pirates are still terrorizing the seas of Southeast Asia, capturing boats and stealing their cargo. In March 1991, a big oil tanker disappeared off the Philippines. This was almost certainly the work of pirates.

Boats are the main form of transport. Rivers provide links between small communities.

Notched tree trunks or ladders are used to get down to the water level.

AUSTRALASIA & OCEANIA

Most Australians live in big cities like Sydney, the capital of New South Wales. Both Australia and New Zealand are big economic powers, trading mainly with Asia and the United States. By contrast, many Pacific islanders of Oceania live in isolated communities that have little contact with the outside world.

Emergency!
The Royal Flying Doctor Service is a lifesaver for people living in remote parts of Australia. Few patients are more than a two-hour flight away from a hospital.

Australian Megamix
British settlers first came to Australia about 200 years ago, but in the last 50 years there have been many new arrivals from other parts of Europe and Asia.

A large number of Australians have British ancestors.

New European arrivals include many Greeks.

Many Italians moved to Australia after the Second World War.

The majority of Australians share a love of the outdoors, and live by the sea.

Aboriginal Art
Aboriginal peoples were the first to settle in Australia, over 40,000 years ago. They have strong artistic traditions, and Aboriginal art is now sold around the world, making much needed money for their communities.

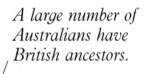

Nauru

New Zealand

Papua New Guinea

Solomon Islands

Tonga

Tuvalu

Vanuatu

Western Samoa

Teaching in Tonga

Tonga is one of the independent nations among the Pacific islands of Oceania. English and Tongan are the two official languages for the small population of 95,000. In Tonga, children have to go to school between the ages of six and fourteen.

First People

These people were some of the first settlers in Australasia and Oceania.

Pacific islander

Papua New Guinea tribesman

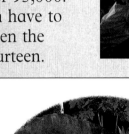

Stone Money

Some Pacific island tribal traditions have not changed for thousands of years. The people of Yap island still use stones like this one as money when they make important property deals.

This boy has Vietnamese parents. English is his second language, just as it is for one in eight other Australians.

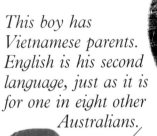

This girl's parents are Chinese. Many Australians are of Asian descent.

Rugby Dance

The Maoris settled in New Zealand about 1,000 years ago. The New Zealand rugby team, the All Blacks, has borrowed some Maori traditions. They use an old Maori war chant, called a haka, to get them in the mood for matches.

Surfing is popular along the coast of Australia.

Maori woman

Aboriginal tribesman

47

GLOSSARY

Ancestor Someone you are related to, who lived and died a very long time ago, before your grandparents were born.

Apartheid A way of organizing society that keeps different races apart.

Civil war War between different groups of people living in the same country.

Civilization The beliefs, customs and way of life of the people living in a particular time or place.

Communism A political system in which the state controls all wealth, property, industry and trade.

Democracy A kind of government, elected by the people to make decisions for the people.

Economy The way a country's goods and services are made, shared out and then used.

Employment Jobs that people do to earn a living.

Ethnic group A group, or tribe, of people who share the same language, religion, customs and ancestors.

Government The group of people in charge of a country. A government's duties include passing laws, controlling trade and looking after relations with other countries.

Nomad Member of a tribe that wanders from place to place, usually looking for pasture for animals.

Politics The work of a government in the running of a country.

Population People who live in a particular place.

Revolution A rebellion that defeats the government of a country and puts another one in its place.

Society The organization of a group of people living together in a community or a country.

Tradition A belief, custom or habit that has been passed down from one generation to another over a very long period of time.

WORLD RELIGIONS

Buddhist Someone who follows the teachings of Buddha. Buddhists worship in temples.

Christian Someone who follows the teachings of Jesus Christ. Christians worship in churches.

Hindu Someone who follows Hinduism, a religion based on holy writings, which include the Vedas. Hindus worship in temples.

Jew A descendant of the ancient tribes of Israel. A Jew may also follow Judaism, a religion based on the teachings of the Bible. Jews worship in synagogues.

Muslim Someone who follows Islam, a religion based on the words of God as spoken to the prophet Muhammad and written down in the Koran. Muslims worship in mosques.

Orthodox Church A group of churches, including those of eastern Europe and northern Eurasia.

Pilgrimage A special journey to a holy place.

Protestant A Christian who does not belong to the Roman Catholic or Orthodox Church.

Religion The belief in and worship of a god or gods.

Roman Catholic A member of the Christian Church that has the Pope as its head.

Shintoism A religion like Buddhism, based in Japan.

Shrine A place where a holy object is kept, where people go to worship a god or saint.

Temple A place of worship for ancient civilizations and many of today's non-Christian religions.

Acknowledgments
The Flying Sneaker courtesy Productions La Fête Inc., Montreal, Canada. Director: Bretislav Pojar, Still Photographer: Ivan Vit; *Dracula* by Bram Stoker published in Penguin Classics, 1986. Reproduced by permission of Penguin Books Ltd.
Photography:
Andy Crawford; Steve Gorton; Tim Kelley; Dave King; Ray Moller; David Murray; Tim Ridley; John Swift, The Colour Company; Andreas von Einsiedel.
Illustrations:
Brian Delf; Roy Flooks; Nick Harris; Trevor Hill; Adam Hook; Aziz Khan; Stuart Lafford; Linden Artists; Jane Pickering; Sebastian Quigley; Eric Thomas; Brian Watson; Steve Weston.
Thanks to:
African Music Agency; Norrie Carr Child Model Agency; Lorenz Hartman; Michael and Megan Jackson; Japanese furniture courtesy of Ken Morita; Murakami family; Tony Pham; Anastasia Phillips; Scallywags Child Model Agency; Vespa from Simon Tynam, Scootabout, London; Japanese food courtesy of Mr Tukuo, Musha Japan Teppan Grill Restaurant, London.

Picture credits
A.F.P. Photo, Paris: Mufti Munir FCc, 5cl, 43cra; **R.W. & J.A. Ainger:** 27bc; **Bryan & Cherry Alexander:** BCtc, 4cr, 20clb, 21tl; **Allsport:** Russell Cheyne 47cr; **Art Directors:** 8c, 29tc; **A.S.A.P:** Yasha Mazur 35tl; **Australian Picture Library:** 25r; **BFI Stills, Posters & Designs:** 32tr; **British Museum:** 13cra; **Bruce Coleman Ltd:** Leonard Lee Rue III 19bl; **Colorsport:** 25crb; **James Davis Worldwide:** 44cla; **Derngate Theatre, Northampton:** 36tr; **Ebenezer Pictures:** Jeremy Browne 2tl, 39crb; **Mary Evans Picture Library:** 13cl, 30clb; **Fotograff:** Patricia Aithie 23crb; **Focus, Argentina:** 14-5; **Robert Harding Picture Library:** FCtc, 2bl, 9cl, 18cla, 20tr, 26cla, 28tr, 42clb, 43crb, Bildagentur Schuster/Meier 33bl, Philip Craven FCtcr, 5bl, 36-7c, Gavin Hellier 41bc, Walter Rawlings 24cb, Christopher Rennie 37c, Adam Woolfitt 24-5bc, 42cla; **Michael Holford:** 29bl; **Hutchison Library:** 17tl, Sarah Errington 19tl, Stephen Pern 37cl, John Ryle 14cl; **The Image Bank:** Derek Berwin 20c, Ira Block 46cl, Andy Caulfield 25cl, Fotoworld 31cl, Andrea Pistolesi FCb, 12b, Barrie Pokeach 4cl, 10br, Steve Proehl 41tl, Harald Sund 39cb, Dag Sundberg 21c; **Images Colour Library:** 23tc, 46cla; **Impact Photos:** Sergio Dorantes 13tl, Alain Le Garsmeur 38tr, Gideon Mendel 19br, Michael Mirecki 27tc; **Legoland, Denmark:** 21cl; **Magnum Photos Ltd:** Abbas FCcla, 16tr, 43c, Eve Arnold 5tr, 38-9, 39c, Bruno Barbey 27c, Fred Mayer 27bl, James Nactwey 13cr, Chris Steele Perkins 4bl, 15c, Raghu Rai 1c, 42-3; ©**National Geographic Society:** Wilbur E.Garrett 6cl; **Network Photographers:** Nikolai Ignatiev 6tr, 36cl, Justin Leighton 30cla, Barry Lewis 5cl, 32b, 33cr, Paul Lowe 34cla, Dod Miller 23tl, Laurie Sparham 33cr; **Panos:** spine t, 19tr; **Picturepoint Ltd:** 17ca; ©**John Reader 1994:** 4cra, 5crb, 15cra, 16clb, 18cr, b, 21tc, 27tl, 34bc, 34-5c, 42c, cb, 45tr, 47c; **Retna Pictures Ltd:** John Welsby 29c; **Rex FeaturesLtd:** Michael Friedel 28cl, Stevens/Zihnioglu/Sipa Press 29cla, Stills/Pat/Arnal 24cr; **Royal Geographical Society:** 7tc; **Schwangau/Ostallgau,Germany:** Tanner Nesselwang 30bl; **Science Photo Library:** David Vaughn 7c, Vanessa Vick 7cr; **Frank Spooner Pictures Ltd:** Gamma/Vlastimir Shone FCcl, 36clb, 37bc, Graham/Liaison Gamma 24cla; **Still Pictures:** Bryan & Cherry Alexander 21cr, Nigel Dickinson 44c; **Tony Stone Images:** BC tl, 3r, 8cr, 11cr, 12cla, 12cr, 22cl, 31cra, 39cra, Paul Berger 45cla, Paul Chesley 40cl, 41cra, cr, 45cl, Brian Chittock 46tr, Robert Frerck 26b, Alain Le Garsmeur 38cb, Margaret Gowan 38c, David Hanson 4cl, 10bc, David Hiser 13c, 47tc, Arnulf Husmo 21b, Olaf Soot BCtr, 4clb, 13bl, Bob Thomason endpaper, Nabeel Turner 5bc, 35cr; **Sygma:** J.Andanson 4br, 25tl, Arthur Grace 33cla, Antoine Gyori 32cl, Jon Jones 19cl, A.Nogues 23c; **Telegraph Colour Library:** Colorific!/ Claus/Camara Tres 14bl, Meyer Roger Ressmeyer/Wheeler 11tl; **Masterfile/Hans Blohm 3c, 7bl, 9cla, cra, John Foster 9tl, J.A.Kraulis 8cla, V.C.L. 28br;** **Vu Agence:** Cristina Garcia Rodero 26cr; **Zefa:** 4c, 11bl, 15ca, 34cl, Damm 28cla, Davies 22tr, Goebel 7tl, Maroon 11crb, Schlenker 14cla.

tl - **top left**   t - **top centre**   tr - **top right**   r - **right**   bl - **bottom left**   bc - **bottom centre**   br - **bottom right**   cra - **centre right above**
cr - **centre right**   cb - **centre below**   crb - **centre right below**   cla - **centre left above**   cl - **centre left**   clb - **centre left below**   c - **centre**   b - **below**

INDEX

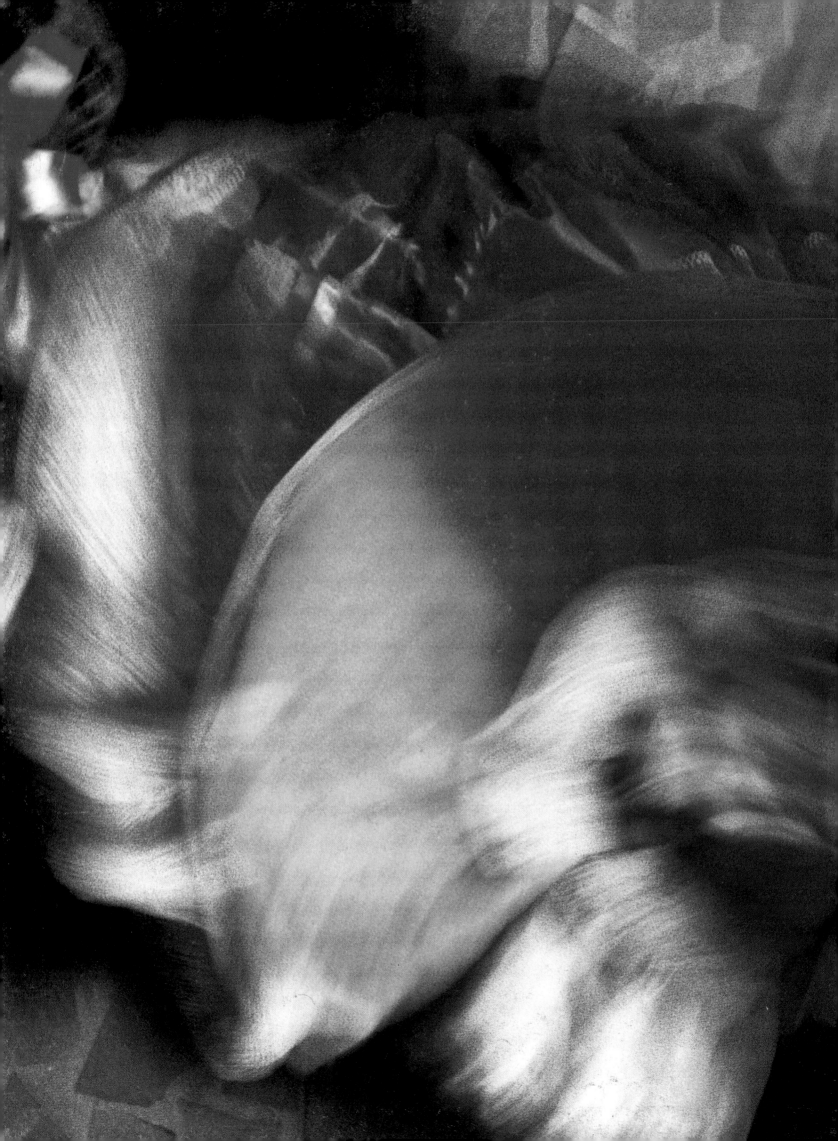